LETTING GO OF CRITICIZING OTHERS

OTHER BOOKS BY SUSAN GAMMAGE

LETTING GO OF CRITICIZING OTHERS

A BAHÁ'Í PERSPECTIVE

Susan Gammage

Muskoka
www.ninestarsolutions.com

© Susan Gammage 2013
All rights reserved

ISBN: 978-0-9936776-2-5

DEDICATION

For Vera and Peter

And for
Val and Karl

And for
Michael and Sarah

And for
Chris

And With Profound Gratitude to the Divine Physician

TABLE OF CONTENTS

WHAT IS FAULT-FINDING, BLAME AND ACCUSATION?

Let's start with a quote from 'Abdu'l-Bahá:

> The Cause of God hath never had any place for
> denouncing others as infidel or profligate, nor
> hath it allowed anyone to humiliate or belittle
> another. Contend and wrangle not with any
> man, and seek ye not the abasement of any soul.
> Disparage not anyone's name, and wish no harm
> upon anyone. Defile not your tongues with
> calumny, and engage ye not in backbiting. Lift
> not the veil from the doings of others, and so
> long as a person professeth to be steadfast,
> remonstrate not with him, nor expose him.
> ('Abdu'l-Bahá, quoted in the Universal House of
> Justice, 2001 Apr 18, Clarification of Various
> Issues Raised by Provisional Translations, p. 2)

In this definition, 'Abdu'l-Bahá tells us it includes:

- denouncing
- humiliating and belittling
- contending and wrangling
- seeking the abasement of another
- disparaging anyone's name

- wishing harm
- defiling your tongue with calumny
- engaging in backbiting
- exposing the doings of others

Here is some of what the Bahá'í Writings have to teach about the various forms of fault-finding:

Abase:

> In a number of earlier religious Dispensations and in certain cultures the kissing of the hand of a religious figure or of a prominent person was expected as a mark of reverence and deference to such persons and as a token of submission to their authority. Bahá'u'lláh prohibits the kissing of hands and, in His Tablets, He also condemns such practices as prostrating oneself before another person and other forms of behaviour that abase one individual in relation to another. (*The Kitáb-i-Aqdas*, Note 57, p. 193)

Acrimony

> For Bahá'ís to go further than this, by engaging in acrimonious debate, much less by reflecting on the character of others, would be to cross the line that separates legitimate defence of the Faith from contention. (The Universal House of Justice, 1999 Nov 22, Defending the Cause against its Opponents, Bahá'í library online)

Belittle:

> The honored members must with all freedom express their own thoughts, and it is in no wise permissible for one to belittle the thought of another… (Shoghi Effendi, *Baha'i Administration*, p. 22)

Calumny:

> The individual must be educated to such a high degree that he would rather have his throat cut than tell a lie, and would think it easier to be slashed with a sword or pierced with a spear than to utter calumny or be carried away by wrath. (*Selections from the Writings of 'Abdu'l-Bahá*, p. 136)

Contend:

> Beware lest ye contend with any one, nay, strive to make him aware of the truth with kindly manner and most convincing exhortation. (*Gleanings from the Writings of Baha'u'llah*, p. 278)

> The worldwide undertakings on which the Cause of God is embarked are far too significant, the need of the peoples of the world for the Message of Bahá'u'lláh far too urgent, the perils facing mankind far too grave, the progress of events far too swift, to permit His followers to

squander their time and efforts in fruitless contention. Now, if ever, is the time for love among the friends, for unity of understanding and endeavor, for self-sacrifice and service by Bahá'ís in every part of the world. (The Universal House of Justice, 1992 Dec 10, Issues Related to the Study of the Bahá'í Faith, p. 28. Ocean Database)

Criticism:

Vicious criticism is indeed a calamity. But its root is lack of faith in the system of Bahá'u'lláh, i.e., the Administrative Order -- and lack of obedience to Him -- for He has forbidden it! If the Bahá'ís would follow the Bahá'í laws . . . all this waste of strength through criticizing others could be diverted into cooperation and achieving the Plan. (Written on behalf of Shoghi Effendi, *Messages to the Antipodes*, p.277)

Denounce:

Denounce ye not one another, ere the Day-Star of ancient eternity shineth forth above the horizon of His sublimity. We have created you from one tree and have caused you to be as the leaves and fruit of the same tree, that haply ye may become a source of comfort to one another. Regard ye not others save as ye regard your own selves, that no feeling of aversion may prevail amongst you so as to shut you out from Him Whom God shall make manifest on the Day of Resurrection. It behooveth you all to be one indivisible people; thus should ye return unto Him Whom God shall make manifest. (*Selections from the Writings of the Bab*, p. 127)

The Cause of God hath never had any place for denouncing others . . . nor hath it allowed anyone to humiliate or belittle another. Contend and wrangle not with any man, and seek ye not the abasement of any soul. Disparage not anyone's name, and wish no harm upon anyone. Defile not your tongues with calumny, and engage ye not in backbiting. Lift not the veil from the doings of others, and so long as a person professeth to be steadfast, remonstrate not with him, nor expose him. ('Abdu'l-Bahá, quoted in the Universal House of Justice, 2001 Apr 18, Clarification of Various Issues Raised by Provisional Translations, p. 2)

Disparage:

. . . abstain from criticizing and disparaging the manners, customs and beliefs of other individuals, peoples and nations. (Shoghi Effendi, *The Compilation of Compilations*, Vol 2, p. 348)

Exposing the Faults of Others:

Magnify not the faults of others that thine own
faults may not appear great . . . (Bahá'u'lláh, *The
Hidden Words,* Persian #44)

Fault-Finding:

On no subject are the Bahá'í teachings more
emphatic than on the necessity to abstain from
fault-finding and backbiting while being ever
eager to discover and root out our own faults
and overcome our own failings. (Written on
behalf of Shoghi Effendi, *Lights of Guidance,* #306,
p. 88)

Harm:

I hope that each one of you will become just, and
direct your thoughts towards the unity of
mankind; that you will never harm your
neighbours nor speak ill of any one; that you will
respect the rights of all men, and be more
concerned for the interests of others than for your
own. ('Abdu'l-Bahá, *Paris Talks,* p. 160)

Humiliate:

On page 346 of his book Abdu'l-Baha H.M. Balyuzi
recounts the story of a prince who had persecuted the
Bahá'ís in Yazd but who, years later, approached 'Abdu'l-
Bahá:

"He was now a broken man and an exile, seemingly contrite, asking for forgiveness. He threw himself at 'Abdu'l-Bahá's feet, but 'Abdu'l-Bahá would not permit him to humiliate himself."

Wrangling:

They must in every matter search out the truth and not insist upon their own opinion, for stubbornness and persistence in one's views will lead ultimately to discord and wrangling and the truth will remain hidden. (*Selections from the Writings of 'Abdu'l-Bahá*, p. 88)

Fault-Finding

Fault-finding is defined as petty or nagging criticism, which can include the following synonyms: Hair-splitting, hard to please, hypercritical, nagging, niggling, nit-picking, quibbling, acrimonious, cantankerous, contrary, crabby, cross, demanding, disparaging, exacting, finicky, irritable, peevish, perverse, petulant, sarcastic, testy, touchy, pick holes in, showing disapproval with the lifting of an eyebrow, sceptical, put off, exaggerated focus on shortcomings.
It could include:

- Someone removed from a given situation who thinks he could do a better job of directing it than those actually in charge.

- A giver of unsolicited advice or criticism

- One who tries to direct a situation which is not his responsibility and over which he has no real control (back seat driver)

- One who criticizes the actions or decisions of others after the fact, and uses hindsight to offer his opinions on what should have been done. ("You should have . . .")

- One who destroys the credibility or reputation of another

- One who blames someone else for a failing of which he is also, and usually more, guilty (usually implies the presence of an unjustified holier-than-thou attitude on the part of the accuser as in "the pot calling the kettle black").

When I first started looking at this material, I didn't think I was a "fault-finder", but then when I looked at some of the synonyms, I began to cringe. Two things stood out:

1. Showing disapproval with the lifting of an eyebrow was how I parented my son, to prevent myself from perpetrating the physical abuse done to me as a child. He called it my "owl look". When he was an adult, he told me he wished I had spanked him instead, because it wouldn't have hurt as much!

2. I'm currently working with a webmaster to put up
    several new websites (Bahá'í Quotes, Stories and
    Prayers). Neither of us is gifted in design, so he
    does something and then I find fault (nit-pick,
    pick holes in, focus on shortcomings). I know
    from past experiences like this, that I can be very
    demanding and exacting.

My hunch is that if you go back and look at the list again,
you will be able to find ways in which you find fault as
well, since it seems to be very pervasive in our Western
culture. It is also our worst characteristic:

> The most hateful characteristic of man is fault-
> finding. ('Abdu'l-Bahá, *Lights of Guidance*, p. 91)

Blame

Blame goes one step further. It is the act of censuring
(vehement expression of disapproval); holding someone
responsible; making negative statements about an
individual or group that their action or actions are socially
or morally irresponsible; the opposite of praise.

Synonyms include: reproach, reprove, reprehend,
criticize, censure, condemn, scold and rebuke.

We constantly consciously and unconsciously find fault
and make judgments about other people, apportioning
blame. Our basis for judging others may be partly
ingrained, negative and rigid indicating some degree of
grandiosity or feelings that we know best how something
ought to be done.

Blaming is also a way of devaluing others. The end result is that the blamer feels superior. Others are seen as less worthwhile making the blamer "perfect". Off-loading blame means putting the other person down by emphasizing his or her flaws.

Here is some of what the Bahá'í Writings have to teach about the various forms of blaming:

Blame:

> It behoveth you, therefore, to attach blame to no one except to yourselves, for the things ye have committed, if ye but judge fairly. (*Gleanings from the Writings of Bahá'u'lláh*, p. 222-223)

Censure:

> Refrain from censure and from slander, and leave him in the Hand of God. (*'Abdu'l-Bahá, Selections from the Writings of 'Abdu'l-Bahá*, p. 315)

Disapproval:

> Even if you are doing nothing deliberately to discourage such freedom, their accumulated impression of institutional disapproval, however derived, and their fear of criticism are, to a considerable extent, inhibiting their exercise of initiative. (Universal House of Justice to the National Spiritual Assembly of the Bahá'ís of the

United States, May 19 1994, paragraph 48. Bahá'í
Library Online)

Reproach:

Generally the speech of reproach and rebuke is
rather too severe for the people and would be
heartbreaking to them. ('Abdu'l-Bahá, *Some
Answered Questions*, p. 167)

O army of God! Beware lest ye harm any soul, or
make any heart to sorrow; lest ye wound any
man with your words, be he known to you or a
stranger, be he friend or foe. ... Beware, beware,
lest ye offend the feelings of another, even
though he be an evil-doer, and he wish you ill.
(*Selections from the Writings of Abdu'l-Baha*, p. 73)

Condemn:

All religions teach that we should love one
another; that we should seek out our own
shortcomings before we presume to condemn
the faults of others, that we must not consider
ourselves superior to our neighbours! We must
be careful not to exalt ourselves lest we be
humiliated. ('Abdu'l-Bahá, *Paris Talks*, p. 147)

Accusation

Accusing is similar. It involves saying that someone has done something wrong or illegal even though this has not been proved. It can be a declaration of fault or blame against another. It can charge falsely or with malicious intent or attack the good name and reputation of someone and usually involves finger pointing.

Synonyms include: to cast aspersions, besmirch, defame, smirch, denigrate, sully, smear, indict, denounce, attribute to, hold responsible for, censure, incriminate, condemn, calumny (a false and malicious statement designed to injure the reputation of someone or something), slander (a malicious, false, and defamatory statement or report) and vilify (speak evil of, to lower in worth or value)

> We should therefore, as tactfully as possible, but yet firmly, do our utmost to prevent others from making accusations or complaints against others in our presence. (Written on behalf of Shoghi Effendi, *Lights of Guidance*, #325, p. 94)

> It is particularly important to refrain from making unfavourable remarks or statements concerning the friends and the loved ones of God, inasmuch as any expression of grievance, of complaint or backbiting is incompatible with the requirements of unity and harmony and would dampen the spirit of love, fellowship and nobility. (*Bahíyyih Khánum*, p. 195)

Here is what the Bahá'í Writings say about the various forms of accusation:

Defame:

> Woe betide every slanderer and defamer.
> (*Tablets of Bahá'u'lláh*, p. 219)

Denounce:

> The Guardian wishes me to draw the attention of the friends through you that they should be very careful in their public utterances not to mention any political figures-either side with them or denounce them. (Written on behalf of Shoghi Effendi, *Lights of Guidance*, #1440 p. 442)

> Denounce ye not one another, ere the Day-Star of ancient eternity shineth forth above the horizon of His sublimity. (*Selections from the Writings of the Báb*, p. 127)

Censure:

> Does not 'Abdu'l-Bahá wish us, as He looks down upon us with loving expectation from His glorious Station, to obliterate as much as possible all traces of censure, of conflicting

discussions, of cooling remarks, of petty unnecessary observations that impede the onward march of the Cause, that damp the zeal of the firm believer and detract from the sublimity of the Bahá'í Cause in the eyes of the inquirer? (Shoghi Effendi, *Baha'i Administration*, p. 19)

Therefore it is incumbent upon the members of the exalted Spiritual Assembly to exercise the utmost care with firm determination and not to allow the doors of complaint and grievance to be opened, or permit any of the friends to indulge in censure and backbiting. Whoever sets himself to do so, even though he be the very embodiment of the Holy Spirit, should realize that such behaviour would create disruption among the people of Bahá and would cause the standard of sedition to be raised. (*Bahíyyih Khánum*, p. 195)

Calumny: (means slander, defamation, libel, lie, misrepresent):

The individual must be educated to such a high degree that he would rather have his throat cut than tell a lie, and would think it easier to be slashed with a sword or pierced with a spear than to utter calumny or be carried away by wrath. (*Selections from the Writings of 'Abdu'l-Bahá*, pp. 136-137)

...against calumny there is no defense . . . having no helper, assistant nor shelter from the sword of accusation and the teeth of calumny, save God! (*Tablets of 'Abdu'l-Bahá v2*, p. 379)

Slander:

Henceforward everyone should utter that which is meet and seemly, and should refrain from slander, abuse and whatever causeth sadness in men. (*Tablets of Bahá'u'lláh*, pp. 219-220)

Woe betide every slanderer and defamer. (*Tablets of Bahá'u'lláh*, p. 219)

Ignoring gossip and slander is a positive, constructive and healing action helpful to the community, the gossiper and to the persons slandered. (Universal House of Justice, *Developing Distinctive Bahá'í Communities*, p. 16.38)

Vilify: (means criticize, belittle)

It is not, however, permissible to strike a child, or vilify him, for the child's character will be totally perverted if he be subjected to blows or verbal abuse. (*Selections from the Writings of 'Abdu'l-Bahá*, p. 125)

Why We Do It

Some people spend their lives looking for something or someone to attack or blame. They're always looking at the negative or the dark side of life. We can never feel peaceful around them, because we're always waiting to be the next target of their negativity. We know we will fail them, and let them down, just as they've been let down by everyone before. It's hard to trust when we're protecting ourselves from their condemnation.

So why do we attack and blame others? Why do we gossip and backbite?

It feels good! We don't feel so alone. We feel heard. We feel relieved. We even sometimes get answers that make our problems lighter.

All three (fault-finding, blame and accusation) involve an element of judgement. The motives for all of them are to eliminate the other person by proving you are right and "they" are wrong. Most of the time, all three need an audience, which leads us to both gossip and backbiting. All of it comes from our lower nature.

> The Bahá'ís must learn to forget personalities
> and to overcome the desire - so natural in people
> - to take sides and fight about it. (Written on
> behalf of Shoghi Effendi, *The Light of Divine
> Guidance v I*, p. 152)

In the article on Fault-Finding in the blog "Living Life
Fully",[1] the author (unknown) says:

> It's easy to find fault in things--far too easy for
> most of us. Somehow, the flaws are far more
> easy to see than the bigger picture, than the
> amount of work and thought and preparation
> have gone into a particular piece of work. Think
> about it--if someone just painted his or her house
> and missed a spot, what's the first thing we
> see? If someone just cooked us dinner and used
> a bit too much salt, what's the first thing we
> notice when we put the food into our mouths?
> And if we do notice the bare spot on the house,
> aren't we doing the person a favor by pointing it
> out? And if the food's too salty we may not be
> able to eat it, so we'll definitely need to explain
> why.
>
> Many of us carry this tendency to extremes,
> though. Many people feel that they need to tell

---

[1] http://www.livinglifefully.com/faultfinding.htm

everyone about every little fault that they find in
every situation. They feel that they're doing
people favors by pointing out what they see as
flaws and problems, even though they may not
be in a position in which people expect them to
find mistakes. And when they do so, they risk
hurting people greatly.

Fault-finding, blame and accusation are related to
bitterness, because bitterness is often what lies behind it.
It is our lower nature's job to cause us to accuse others and
to hook into other people so they can accuse us. Our
lower nature wants us to think the worst of others and
blame and accuse them, so that we stay trapped in the
prison of self, far removed from our true station which is
to know and worship God.

It can happen at three levels – criticism against ourselves
(by ourselves and others); against others (by us) and
against God. Let's look at each of these individually.

CRITICIZING OURSELVES

It's often said that we're our worst enemy, and in this case, when we find fault, blame and accuse ourselves, this is certainly true. When Bahá'u'lláh told us to:

> Bring thyself to account each day . . . (*The Hidden Words*, Arabic #31)

He wasn't asking us to only look at our negative qualities. It took me years to understand that accountants ("account"ants) look at both the debits (negatives) and credits (positives), and both are needed to balance the books.

Bahá'u'lláh tells us to be moderate in all things:

> In all circumstances they should conduct themselves with moderation. (*Lights of Guidance*, #1004, p. 295)

When we just look at our negatives, we are not being moderate.

He also tells us

> Whatsoever passeth beyond the limits of moderation will cease to exert a beneficial

influence. (*Gleanings from the Writings of Bahá'u'lláh*, p. 216)

So if we are overly critical of ourselves, we aren't being moderate and nothing good can come of it.

Instead of always looking at our shortcomings, Shoghi Effendi suggests we add up our accomplishments:

> He urges you to persevere and add up your accomplishments, rather than to dwell on the dark side of things. (Written on behalf of Shoghi Effendi, *Unfolding Destiny*, p. 457)

Blaming Ourselves

There are two main types of self-blame:

1. Undeserved blame based on <u>actions</u>. Those who experience this kind of self-blame feel that they should have done something differently and therefore feel at fault.

    We might have thoughts such as:

    - Remember what you did 20 years ago?
    - Why did you do that?
    - What were you thinking?
    - Nothing will ever be right again because of that bad decision you made
    - I've made so many mistakes that can't be undone
    - I've wasted my life

When life doesn't go the way we want, we
convince ourselves that God is still punishing us;
even for sins we've already repented for and
turned away from. We still feel guilty and
continue to condemn ourselves. We can't let go,
trusting that we don't have to ask forgiveness over
and over again. It's just another way to continue
abasement. God forgave us the first time we
asked His forgiveness.

2.   Undeserved blame based on <u>character</u>. Victims
      who experience this kind of self-blame feel there is
      something inherently wrong with them.

      We might have thoughts such as:

        • I don't belong
        • Nobody likes me
        • It's all my fault
        • I'm such a sinner
        • I'm no good
        • I can't do anything right
        • I'm not worthy to be a Bahá'í
        • I'm stupid
        • I don't fit in
        • I don't look good enough
        • I have nothing to offer
        • There's no reason for me to participate in
          Bahá'í community life
        • I might as well be dead
        • I'll never have anything
        • I'll never be somebody

Victims of abuse (some studies suggest that this includes ¼ of the earth's population), for example, often feel responsible for causing negative feelings in the abuser towards them and then get trapped in a self-image of victimization which includes a pervasive sense of helplessness, passivity, loss of control, pessimism, negative thinking, strong feelings of guilt, shame, remorse, self-blame and depression. This way of thinking can lead to hopelessness and despair.[2]

Counselling found to be helpful in reducing self-blame includes support and education including cognitive restructuring (learning to take the facts and form a logical conclusion from them that is less influenced by shame or guilt).[3] Reading the Bahá'í Writings is the best way to educate ourselves about what is true, and helps us reframe our experiences and beliefs.

We often experience self-condemnation when we don't know how God sees us. God created us in His image:

> God hath created all humankind in His own image, and after His own likeness. (*Selections from the Writings of 'Abdu'l-Bahá*, p. 79)

And because He loved us:

> I knew My love for thee; therefore I created thee, have engraved on thee Mine image and revealed

---

[2] http://en.wikipedia.org/wiki/Blame
[3] http://en.wikipedia.org/wiki/Blame

> to thee My beauty. (Bahá'u'lláh, *The Hidden Words*, Arabic #3)

He created us with a lower nature:

> Today all people are immersed in the world of nature. That is why thou dost see jealousy, greed, the struggle for survival, deception, hypocrisy, tyranny, oppression, disputes, strife, bloodshed, looting and pillaging, which all emanate from the world of nature. (*Selections from the Writings of Abdu'l-Baha*, p. 206)

> All the imperfections found in the animal are found in man. In him there is antagonism, hatred and selfish struggle for existence; in his nature lurk jealousy, revenge, ferocity, cunning, hypocrisy, greed, injustice and tyranny. So to speak, the reality of man is clad in the outer garment of the animal, the habiliments of the world of nature, the world of darkness, imperfections and unlimited baseness. (Abdu'l-Baha, *Foundations of World Unity*, p. 110)

Now that we know how we were created, there's no need to judge ourselves too harshly when we find ourselves slipping into our lower nature.

When we immerse ourselves in the Ocean of Bahá'u'lláh's Writings and strive to implement them, we will achieve our true purpose in life (which is to know and worship

God). We will be able to overcome our lower nature and
be able to:

> Rise then unto that for which thou wast created.
> (Bahá'u'lláh, *The Hidden Words*, Arabic #22)

CRITICISM FROM OTHERS

The first thing to know is that others <u>will</u> attack us! We can expect this. 'Abdu'l-Bahá tells us:

> All who stand up in the cause of God will be persecuted and misunderstood. It hath ever been so, and will ever be. Let neither enemy nor friend disturb your composure, destroy your happiness, deter your accomplishment. Rely wholly upon God. Then will persecution and slander make you the more radiant. The designs of your enemies will rebound upon them. They, not you, will suffer. ('Abdu'l-Bahá, *The Compilation of Compilations v1*, #308, p. 155)

> A large multitude of people will arise against you, showing oppression, expressing contumely and derision, shunning your society, and heaping upon you ridicule. ('Abdu'l-Bahá, *The Compilation of Compilations v1*, #269, p. 137)

> Therefore, my purpose is to warn and strengthen you against accusations, criticisms, revilings, and derision . . . Be not disturbed by them. They are the very confirmation of the Cause, the very source of upbuilding to the Movement. ('Abdu'l-Bahá, *Promulgation of Universal Peace*, p. 429)

Fortunately (or unfortunately!), most of us have already experienced blame, judgement and fault-finding, starting when we were children. Our parents might have said thoughtless things like:

- You're no good
- You'll never amount to anything.
- You never do anything right

Then we might have gone to school and heard things like:

- You're lazy
- You're stupid

These negative comments might become so familiar we might have married someone who tells us the same things in the form of:

- You don't work hard enough
- You don't look good enough
- You can't do anything right

When we listen to these lies for years and believe them (because they come from people who are meant to love and protect us), we take them in and start believing them to be true. When we do, we're taking someone else's sin into every fiber of our being. We need help to stop doing this:

> Women and children must be helped to avoid . . . blaming themselves, and accepting cultural rationales. (Bahá'í International Community, 1994 May 23, *Creating Violence-Free Families*)

I've had several clients in my Bahá'í-inspired life coaching practice, hurt by comments made by other Bahá'í friends and family members. In my role as their life coach, I've pointed out some spiritual principles which can help govern their behaviour. I've compiled a list of their questions, comment and concerns, and quotes from the Bahá'í Writings which address them. Hope it gives you a perspective to help you deal with these issues, which are no doubt occurring in your lives too.

Why do friends criticize and put me down?

> Perhaps the greatest test Bahá'ís are ever subjected to is from each other... (Written on behalf of Shoghi Effendi, *Lights of Guidance*, p. 602, # 2037)

> . . . if we are very sensitive, or if we are in some way brought up in a different environment from the Bahá'ís amongst whom we live, we naturally see things differently and may feel them more acutely; and the other side of it is that the imperfections of our fellow-Bahá'ís can be a great trial to us. (Written on behalf of Shoghi Effendi, *Lights of Guidance*, p. 604, # 2047)

> Generally speaking nine-tenths of the friends' troubles are because they don't do the Bahá'í thing, in relation to each other, to the administrative bodies or in their personal lives. (Shoghi Effendi, *Unfolding Destiny*, p. 454)

How can I behave towards them when they hurt me?

. . . for the sake of the Master they should be ever ready to overlook each other's mistakes, apologize for harsh words they have uttered, forgive and forget. He strongly recommends to you this course of action. (Written on behalf of Shoghi Effendi, *Lights of Guidance*, p. 602, #2037)

. . . often our severest tests come from each other . . . and if they happen, remedy them through love. (Shoghi Effendi, *Unfolding Destiny*, p. 454)

You should not allow the remarks made by the Bahá'ís to hurt or depress you, but should forget the personalities, and arise to do all you can, yourself, to teach the Faith. (Shoghi Effendi, *Unfolding Destiny,* p. 462)

. . . if you close your eyes to the failings of others, and fix your love and prayers upon Bahá'u'lláh, you will have the strength to weather this storm, and will be much better for it in the end, spiritually. Although you suffer, you will gain a maturity that will enable you to be of greater help to both your fellow Bahá'ís and your children. (Written on behalf of Shoghi Effendi, *Lights of Guidance,* p. 604, #2047)

. . . turning a sin-covering eye to the faults of others, and striving in our own inmost selves to purify our lives in accordance with the divine teachings. (*Messages from the Universal House of Justice: 1963-1986*, p. 499, para. 289.2)

1. Great love and patience are needed towards new believers, especially those who have come from very troubled backgrounds. (*Messages from the Universal House of Justice: 1963-1986*, p. 499, para. 289.4)

Concerning the attitude of some Bahá'ís, who seem at times to be insensitive and unsupportive, all we can do is to try to follow the patient example of the Master, bearing in mind that each believer is but one of the servants of the Almighty who must strive to learn and grow. The absence of spiritual qualities, like darkness, has no existence in itself. As the light of spirituality penetrates deep into the hearts, this darkness gradually dissipates and is replaced by virtue. Understanding this, and that the believers are encouraged to be loving and patient with one another, it will be clear that you too are called upon to exercise patience with the friends who demonstrate immaturity, and to have faith that the power of the Word of God will gradually effect a transformation in individual believers and in the Bahá'í community as a whole. (Written on behalf of the Universal House of Justice to an individual believer, 23 October, 1994. Bahá'í Library Online)

What can I do when it's the Assembly who has reacted negatively?

Your letters have been read with great sympathy by the House of Justice. You have written eloquently about the pain and isolation felt by yourself and other believers, particularly women, when faced with a lack of response from those very Assemblies which Bahá'u'lláh has asked us to consider as loving parents. From such bodies, one longs for understanding and, beyond that, for encouragement and love. When we feel that this is missing, our own reactions may include feelings of disillusionment and alienation. In addition, there are other issues which arise within our communities which cannot be dealt with through a decision per se but which require, for their resolution, growth and changes of attitude on the part of the friends. When progress is slow or appears to be blocked, we may feel the urge to distance ourselves from the friends and the institutions, and despite our best intentions we may find ourselves almost involuntarily withdrawing into non-responsive, non-encouraging modes of our own. We must struggle with such promptings from within, setting our sights on the lofty ex-ample set by the Greatest Holy Leaf who, throughout a life replete with severe tests, chose not to take offence at the actions or lack of actions of other souls and, with full and radiant heart, continued to bestow on them love and encouragement. (Written on behalf of the Universal House of Justice, to an individual believer, 25 October, 1994, found in *Violence and Abuse: Reasons and Remedies* p. 64)

As you know, there can be many reasons for Assemblies not to respond to the believers. Undoubtedly, in some cases, it is because the friends and the Assemblies are struggling with issues on the frontier of their spiritual growth. Such a process can lead to tremendous development on both the individual and the collective levels. Sometimes we can facilitate this process of spiritual growth for individuals, and of maturation for Local and National Assemblies, by viewing these situations not as a problem but as opportunities for development. Taking part in this process should be a source of joy to us since we are, in effect, helping to build the kingdom of God on Earth. Nevertheless, patience is needed, particularly when it involves a subject that is close to our hearts, and when it seems that progress on the matter is lagging or has ceased entirely. We must maintain our confidence that the divinely ordained administrative system given to us by Bahá'u'lláh, and the inspiration of the Creative Word, will enable us to rise to these challenges. (Unpublished letter written on behalf of the Universal House of Justice to an individual believer, 25 October, 1994)

Letting Go Of The Hurt

When someone dumps their issues on us in the form of blaming us for something; instead of taking a spiritual bath (realizing it's their sin; and not letting our lower nature take over), we accept it and slide into gossip and backbiting. We tell others about "that mean thing he said about me"; encouraging them to agree with us that "that person is bad" . . . and none of this is from God!

If a bird defecates on us, we go home and wash it off. That's what we need to do with accusations. The spiritual equivalent is to immerse ourselves in the Writings to learn and come back to the truth of who we are. The more we do this, the easier it is to cast off the accusations, because we know who we are.

Bahá'u'lláh tells us we are noble beings, rich in gems of inestimable value. That's our reality. That's a truth we can hold on to.

> Noble have I created thee . . . (Bahá'u'lláh, *The Hidden Words*, Arabic #22).

> Regard man as a mine rich in gems of inestimable value. (*Gleanings from the Writings of Bahá'u'lláh*, p. 260)

God came to make all things new.

> Immeasurably exalted is the breeze that wafteth from the garment of thy Lord, the Glorified! For lo, it hath breathed its fragrance and made all

> things new! Well it is with them that
> comprehend. (Bahá'u'lláh cited by Shoghi
> Effendi in, *The Promised Day is Come*, p. 46)

When we make mistakes, we can remind ourselves that
we may not be perfect, but we know we're working on
becoming better little by little, day by day, and God sees
every effort we make, so there is no need for self-
condemnation.

> We have graciously accepted thy devotions, thy
> praise, thy teaching work and the services thou
> hast rendered for the sake of this mighty
> Announcement. (*Tablets of Bahá'u'lláh*, p. 245)

> Moreover, although these insignificant amounts
> are not worthy of mention, they are well
> pleasing, since the donors offer them for the sake
> of God. If the offering be but a single grain it is
> regarded as the crowning glory of all the
> harvests of the world. (Bahá'u'lláh, *The
> Compilation of Compilations V 1*, p. 490, 1103)

When someone accuses us of something, there are two
possibilities: either it's true or it's not true. If it's true, we
can make a little adjustment and thank the person for
bringing it to our attention. If it's not true, it's a little more
complicated spiritually because we're dealing with a
betrayal which is similar to grief, so we also have to deal
with rejection and bitterness.

When you're accused of something, it brings up all kinds
of fear: fear of the person who blamed you; fear of other

people finding out; fear of rejection, failure, abandonment
. . . all of which create veils between us and God.

When people slander us, accuse us, act against us (as they
will), the Bahá'í Faith gives us a standard to live up to:

> Grieve not at the things that have befallen Thee,
> for erelong shall God raise up a people who will
> see with their own eyes and will recall Thy
> tribulations. (Bahá'u'lláh, *The Summons of the
> Lord of Hosts*, p. 17)

> Withhold Thy pen from the mention of Thine
> enemies, and bestir it in the praise of the Eternal
> King. (Bahá'u'lláh, *The Summons of the Lord of
> Hosts*, p. 17)

> Bahá'u'lláh has clearly said in His Tablets that if
> you have an enemy, consider him not as an
> enemy. Do not simply be long-suffering; nay,
> rather, love him. Your treatment of him should
> be that which is becoming to lovers. Do not even
> say that he is your enemy. Do not see any
> enemies. Though he be your murderer, see no
> enemy. Look upon him with the eye of
> friendship. Be mindful that you do not consider
> him as an enemy and simply tolerate him, for
> that is but stratagem and hypocrisy. To consider
> a man your enemy and love him is hypocrisy.
> This is not becoming of any soul. You must
> behold him as a friend. You must treat him well.
> This is right. ('Abdu'l-Bahá, *The Promulgation of
> Universal Peace*, p. 267)

Here's a story of how 'Abdu'l-Bahá did it:

> Hear how he treats his enemies. One instance of
> many I have heard will suffice. When the
> Master came to 'Akká there lived there a certain
> man from Afghanistan [Haji Siddiq], an austere
> and rigid Mussulman [Muslim]. To him the
> Master was a heretic. He felt and nourished a
> great enmity towards the Master, and roused up
> others against him. When opportunity offered in
> gatherings of the people, as in the Mosque, he
> denounced him with bitter words.
>
> 'This man,' he said to all, 'is an imposter. Why do
> you speak to him? Why do you have dealings
> with him?' And when he passed the Master on
> the street he was careful to hold his robe before
> his face that his sight might not be defiled. Thus
> did the Afghan. The Master, however, did thus:
> The Afghan was poor and lived in a mosque; he
> was frequently in need of food and clothing. The
> Master sent him both. These he accepted, but
> without thanks. He fell sick. The Master took
> him a physician, food, medicine, money. These,
> also, he accepted; but as he held out one hand
> that the physician might take his pulse, with the
> other he held his cloak before his face that he
> might not look upon the Master. For twenty-four
> years the Master continued his kindnesses and
> the Afghan persisted in his enmity.
>
> Then at last one day the Afghan came to the
> Master's door, and fell down, penitent and
> weeping, at his feet. 'Forgive me, sir!' he cried.

'For twenty-four years I have done evil to you,
for twenty-four years you have done good to me.
Now I know that I have been in the wrong.' The
Master bade him rise, and they became friends.
(Balyuzi, H.M., *'Abdu'l-Bahá*, p. 101)

We don't have to take their accusations, or carry them in
our physical, emotional, psychological beings. We don't
have to have fear, anger, bitterness or self-pity. We don't
have to repay evil for evil, or be affected by another
person's sin. We have a choice to recognize that all of
these are emanating from our lower nature, detach from
them, ask God's forgiveness, forgive ourselves for
entertaining these ideas, and move on with our day. It
really is that simple!

Here are some other ideas:

1. Ignore rebuffs:

    We must never dwell too much on the attitudes
    and feelings of our fellow believers towards us.
    What is most important is to foster love and
    harmony and ignore any rebuffs we may receive;
    in this way the weakness of human nature and
    the peculiarity or attitude of any particular
    person is not magnified, but pales into
    insignificance in comparison with our joint
    service to the Faith we all love. (Written on
    behalf of Shoghi Effendi, *Lights of Guidance*, p.
    116, #397)

2.   Don't worry about the things others say about you:

By all these it is meant that thou must not be sorry and grieved because of these things the papers have written against thee; nay, rather trust in God and be unmoved by either the praise or the false accusations declared by people towards thee, depend entirely on God and exert thyself to serve His holy vineyard. All else save this is but imagination, though it be the praises of all people in thy behalf; because all else is of no result and bears no fruit. (*Tablets of 'Abdu'l-Bahá v1*, p. 158)

Therefore, my purpose is to warn and strengthen you against accusations, criticisms, revilings and derision in newspaper articles or other publications. Be not disturbed by them. They are the very confirmation of the Cause, the very source of upbuilding to the Movement. ('Abdu'l-Bahá, *The Promulgation of Universal Peace*, p. 429)

3.   Show forth love and affection:

The more they deride and blame thee, show thou forth the greater love and affection. Do not look upon their shortcomings. Look thou upon all of them as the people of God and endeavor thou in right-doing and well-meaning. (*Tablets of 'Abdu'l-Bahá v3*, p. 504)

. . . show to alien souls this same loving kindness
ye bestow upon your faithful friends. Should
any come to blows with you, seek to be friends
with him; should any heap his blame upon you,
be ye a healing salve unto his sores; should any
taunt and mock at you, meet him with love.
Should any heap his blame upon you, praise ye
him; should he offer you a deadly poison, give
him the choicest honey in exchange; and should
he threaten your life, grant him a remedy that
will heal him evermore. Should he be pain itself,
be ye his medicine; should he be thorns, be ye
his roses and sweet herbs. (*Selections from the
Writings of 'Abdu'l-Bahá*, p. 34)

4. Seek God's approval instead of worrying about
    what others are saying or doing to hurt us:

    Man must seek to gain the acceptance of God
    and not that of the different classes of men. If
    one is praised and chosen by God, the accusation
    of all the creatures will cause no loss to him; and
    if the man is not accepted in the threshold of
    God, the praise and admiration of all men will
    be of no use to him. (*Tablets of 'Abdu'l-Bahá v1*, p.
    158)

It's not our job to fix the problem or defend ourselves
against their accusations. God sees the truth. God will
take care of the justice. God will protect and defend us if
we'll let Him.

Whatever hath befallen you, hath been for the sake of God. This is the truth, and in this there is no doubt. You should, therefore, leave all your affairs in His Hands, place your trust in Him, and rely upon Him. He will assuredly not forsake you. In this, likewise, there is no doubt. No father will surrender his sons to devouring beasts; no shepherd will leave his flock to ravening wolves. He will most certainly do his utmost to protect his own. If, however, for a few days, in compliance with God's all-encompassing wisdom, outward affairs should run their course contrary to one's cherished desire, this is of no consequence and should not matter. Our intent is that all the friends should fix their gaze on the Supreme Horizon, and cling to that which hath been revealed in the Tablets. (Bahá'u'lláh, The Compilation of Compilations v1, p. 171, #334)

Here's a prayer we can say, asking God to protect us:

O my Lord! Make Thy protection my armor, Thy preservation my shield, humbleness before the door of Thy oneness my guard, and Thy custody and defense my fortress and my abode. ('Abdul-Bahá, *Bahá'í Prayers*, p. 135)

CRITICIZING OTHERS

We accuse others when we think they have something we
think should be ours, whether it's possessions or fame.
These thoughts attack us, causing self-hatred and self-
rejection. Every time we accuse, blame or judge someone,
it's like swallowing poison and hoping it will kill the other
person.

Participating in fault-finding, blame and accusation is not
a good idea, for a couple of reasons:

Our own faults will appear great:

> . . . magnify not the faults of others that thine
> own faults may not appear great . . .
> (Bahá'u'lláh, *The Hidden Words*, Persian #44)

And worse, we'll be accursed of God:

> How couldst thou forget thine own faults and
> busy thyself with the faults of others? Whoso
> doeth this is accursed of Me. (Bahá'u'lláh, *The
> Hidden Words*, Arabic #26)

When we focus on the faults of others, 'Abdu'l-Bahá calls
us "heedless" (which means "careless; thoughtless;
unmindful"):

> Heedless souls are always seeking faults in others. What can the hypocrite know of others' faults when he is blind to his own? ('Abdu'l-Bahá, *The Promulgation of Universal Peace*, p. 244)

The solution lies in becoming aware of and educating ourselves about how our lower nature tricks us into blaming others and drawing us further away from God.

> The root cause of wrongdoing is ignorance, and we must therefore hold fast to the tools of perception and knowledge. Good character must be taught. (*Selections from the Writings of 'Abdu'l-Bahá*, p. 136)

These judgments arise from our lower nature, to keep us isolated and alone, so we can dwell on our wrongs and descend into bitterness and self-pity. They rob us of our identity, ensure we never feel safe and keep us from knowing who we are.

Stop Believing Lies

God gave us life; He created us noble but we have abased ourselves by listening to the lies told to us by ourselves and others: lies that lead us into negativity, fault-finding, blame and accusation. These lies rob us of our life and our peace.

These accusations against ourselves and others are not who we are! They're just negative thoughts coming from our lower nature, and they are lies.

'Abdu'l-Bahá says we don't have to treat liars (including ourselves) kindly, because it encourages them to continue, so recognize these judgments for the lies they are and don't give them anymore room in your inn!

> Kindness cannot be shown the tyrant, the deceiver, or the thief, because, far from awakening them to the error of their ways, it maketh them to continue in their perversity as before. No matter how much kindliness ye may expend upon the liar, he will but lie the more, for he believeth you to be deceived, while ye understand him but too well, and only remain silent out of your extreme compassion. (*Selections from the Writings of Abdu'l-Baha*, p. 158)

It's not easy, as the House of Justice tells us:

> …learning not to concern oneself with the faults of others seems to be one of the most difficult lessons for people to master, and that failing in this is a fertile cause of disputes among Bahá'ís as it is among men and women in general. (Written on behalf of the Universal House of Justice, *Lights of Guidance*, p. 89, 309)

What to Do Instead

Some things we can do instead include focusing on our own lives, so we don't have time or energy to focus on anyone else's:

1. **Know your own shortcomings:**

> As long as a man does not find his own
> faults, he can never become perfect. Nothing
> is more fruitful for man than the knowledge
> of his own shortcomings. The Blessed
> Perfection says, "I wonder at the man who
> does not find his own imperfections."
> ('Abdu'l-Bahá, *The Promulgation of Universal
> Peace*, p. 244)

2. **Look at your own faults and not the faults of others:**

> If the fire of self overcome you, remember
> your own faults and not the faults of My
> creatures, inasmuch as every one of you
> knoweth his own self better than he knoweth
> others. (Bahá'u'lláh, *The Hidden Words*,
> Persian #66)

3. **Plow your own field:** When we're busy focusing on
    our own affairs, we don't have time to dwell on the
    faults of others.

> Each of us is responsible for one life only, and
> that is our own. Each of us is immeasurably
> far from being 'perfect as our heavenly Father
> is perfect' and the task of perfecting our own
> life and character is one that requires all our
> attention, our will- power and energy.
> (Written on behalf of Shoghi Effendi, *Lights of
> Guidance*, p. 92, #318)

If we allow our attention and energy to be taken up in efforts to keep others right and remedy their faults, we are wasting precious time. We are like ploughmen each of whom has his team to manage and his plough to direct, and in order to keep his furrow straight he must keep his eye on his goal and concentrate on his own task. If he looks to this side and that to see how Tom and Harry are getting on and to criticize their ploughing, then his own furrow will assuredly become crooked. (Written on behalf of Shoghi Effendi, *Lights of Guidance*, p. 92, #318)

It is my hope that you may consider this matter, that you may search out your own imperfections and not think of the imperfections of anybody else. Strive with all your power to be free from imperfections. Heedless souls are always seeking faults in others. What can the hypocrite know of others' faults when he is blind to his own? ('Abdu'l-Bahá, *The Promulgation of Universal Peace*, p. 244)

4.   **Get rid of our own imperfections:**

It is my hope that you may consider this matter, that you may search out your own imperfections and not think of the imperfections of anybody else. Strive with all your power to be free from imperfections.

('Abdu'l-Bahá, *The Promulgation of Universal Peace*, p. 244)

Justice

Sometimes when someone injures us, we want to lay charges, but this is not advised:

> As to thine action against the journal which hath libeled thee: It is not at all best to bring action against them, because there is no profit in doing that; nay, it will lead to more sayings of a similar nature. Under these circumstances silence is best. Thou must not be disappointed, sorry or grieved thereat; God will remove all these difficulties. If thou wilt employ thyself in the service (of the Cause of God) the past losses will be recovered and all the troubles will be settled. This is the manifest truth. ('Abdu'l-Bahá, *Tablets of 'Abdu'l-Bahá v1*, p. 158-159)

Even in situations as serious as sexual abuse and murder, pressing charges is discouraged, as we see in the following letters written to individuals. Although this guidance may not apply to every situation, I've given them to you for your consideration. If you have further questions about your situation, please contact the Institutions or the House of Justice.

> At this time there appears to be no substantial reason why you should press charges against your adoptive father, grievous as has been his misuse of your childhood. There seems to be little hazard to any other person from this

behaviour pattern. (From a letter written on behalf of the Universal House of Justice to an individual believer, 22 December, 1981)

You enquire whether you should take action to have your parents charged with murder, following the death of your brother. You should ascertain from a competent lawyer what are your legal obligations in this regard, and follow such requirements. If there are no legal obligations, it is left to your discretion to decide on this matter, in light of the circumstances. However, you might well ask yourself, in the course of this decision-making, what beneficial result is to be gained from such an action, more especially if the action occurred some years ago and if legally-acceptable proof is difficult to establish; you should also weigh carefully the effect this might have on yourself, in the process of re-opening the subject, testifying about it in court, and doubtless incurring the antagonism of your parents. (Universal House of Justice, Recovering from Childhood Trauma, 9 September, 1992. Bahá'í Library Online)

Leave the judging to God because He promises not to forgive anyone's injustice:

I have pledged Myself not to forgive any man's injustice. This is My covenant which I have irrevocably decreed in the preserved tablet and sealed it with My seal of glory. (Bahá'u'lláh, *The Hidden Words*, Persian #64)

Take serious issues to the Institutions (Assemblies or members of the Auxiliary Board). God doesn't want us to be judge and jury. That's the role of the institutions and once you give them your problem it's not yours anymore. It belongs to the Institutions.

> 'Abdu'l-Bahá does not permit adverse criticism of individuals by name in discussion among the friends, even if the one criticizing believes that he is doing so to protect the interests of the Cause. If the situation is of such gravity as to endanger the interests of the Faith, the complaint, as your National Spiritual Assembly has indicated, should be submitted to the Local Spiritual Assembly, or as you state to a representative of the institution of the Counsellors, for consideration and action. In such cases, of course, the name of the person or persons involved will have to be mentioned. (Written on behalf of the Universal House of Justice, *Lights of Guidance*, p. 90, #311)

> There is a tendency to mix up the functions of the Administration and try to apply it in individual relationships, which is abortive, because the Assembly is a nascent House of Justice and is supposed to administer, according to the Teachings, the affairs of the community. But individuals toward each other are governed by love, unity, forgiveness and a sin-covering eye. Once the friends grasp this they will get along much better, but they keep playing Spiritual Assembly to each other and expect the Assembly to behave like an individual....

(Written on behalf of Shoghi Effendi, *Lights of Guidance*, p. 77, #270)

Love the Sinner but Hate the Sin

Now that we don't have to spend time and energy worrying about justice, we can focus it on other things. The first thing to do it to separate the person from the sin, recognizing that their accusation or judgments' are coming from their lower natures, trying to destroy who God created us to be.

> As a devoted believer you are urged to strive to develop forgiveness in your heart toward your parents who have abused you in so disgraceful a manner, and to attain a level of insight which sees them as captives of their lower nature, whose actions can only lead them deeper into unhappiness and separation from God. By this means, you can liberate yourself from the anger to which you refer in your letter. (Universal House of Justice, Recovering from Childhood Trauma, 9 September, 1992. Bahá'í Library Online)

The next is to look towards each other with love and a sin-covering eye. If we fill our hearts with love and ask God to be a channel for His love to the other person, we won't have any space left for fault-finding, blame and accusation:

> But individuals toward each other are governed by love, unity, forgiveness and a sin-covering eye. Once the friends grasp this they will get

along much better.... (Written on behalf of
Shoghi Effendi, *Lights of Guidance*, p. 77, #270)

The antidote to fault-finding, blame and accusation is to
look for the good in others, as we see in the following
quotes:

If a man has ten good qualities and one bad one,
to look at the ten and forget the one; and if a
man has ten bad qualities and one good one, to
look at the one and forget the ten. ('Abdu'l-Bahá,
cited in Bahá'u'lláh and the New Era, p. 83)

It is related that His Holiness Christ . . . one day,
accompanied by His apostles, passed by the
corpse of a dead animal. One of them said: 'How
putrid has this animal become!' The other
exclaimed: 'How it is deformed!' A third cried
out: 'What a stench! How cadaverous looking!'
but His Holiness Christ said: "Look at its teeth!
how white they are!' Consider, that He did not
look at all at the defects of that animal; nay,
rather, He searched well until He found the
beautiful white teeth. He observed only the
whiteness of the teeth and overlooked entirely
the deformity of the body, the dissolution of its
organs and the bad odour.

This is the attribute of the children of the
Kingdom. This is the conduct and the manner of
the real Bahá'ís. I hope that all the believers will
attain to this lofty station. ('Abdu'l-Bahá, *Lights
of Guidance*, p. 91, #312)

One must see in every human being only that
which is worthy of praise. When this is done,
one can be a friend to the whole human race. If,
however, we look at people from the standpoint
of their faults, then being a friend to them is a
formidable task. (*Selections from the Writings of
'Abdul-Bahá*, p. 169, #319)

Instead of gossiping about their faults, 'Abdu'l-Bahá tells
us to praise them without distinction:

Never speak disparagingly of others, but praise
without distinction. ('Abdu'l-Bahá, *The
Promulgation of Universal Peace*, p. 453)

I think "without distinction" here might mean without
saying things like:

- This dinner is great but . . .
- You look beautiful but . . .

And instead of general praise, focus on their virtues
saying things like:

- I appreciate your helpfulness.
- Thank you for your generosity.

CRITICIZING GOD

Everyone tries to make sense of the things that happen to us in our lives. We need the world to make sense, so we create it in our image of what's fair and just. We forget that we can't ever make a plan for the world that's better than God's.

> This is the divine policy, and it is impossible for man to lay the foundation of a better plan and policy than that which God has instituted. ('Abdu'l-Bahá, *The Promulgation of Universal Peace*, p. 107)

> Can humanity conceive a plan and policy better and superior to that of God? It is certain that no matter how capable man may be in origination of plan and organization of purpose, his efforts will be inadequate when compared with the divine plan and purpose; for the policy of God is perfect. Therefore, we must follow the will and plan of God. ('Abdu'l-Bahá, *The Promulgation of Universal Peace*, p. 127)

Often we forget that God's ways are not the same as ours.

> Blessed is the man that hath acknowledged his belief in God and in His signs, and recognized that

> "He shall not be asked of His doings." (*Gleanings from the Writings of Bahá'u'lláh*, p. 86-87)

> He doeth as He doeth, and what recourse have we? He carrieth out His Will, He ordaineth what He pleaseth. Then better for thee to bow down thy head in submission, and put thy trust in the All-Merciful Lord. (*Selections from the Writings of 'Abdu'l-Bahá*, p. 51)

God has a much bigger plan for both us and for the world, than we can ever imagine. Trying to understand it is like a painting trying to understand the painter.

> The working out of God's Major Plan proceeds mysteriously in ways directed by Him alone. (Universal House of Justice, *Messages from the Universal House of Justice: 1963-1986*, p. 127, paragraph #55.5)

By thinking we know what's best, our lower nature tricks us into accusing God. It lets us believe that God is unwilling or unable to help us, withholding some blessing from us while He seems to give blessings freely to everyone else.

We may believe that because we want something, it's God's obligation to give it to us. That kind of thinking is just idle fancy. Just because we want something doesn't mean it's what God wants for us.

We accuse God of withholding things when we think we know how things should be, for example, when bad things happen to good people.

For example, we might think it's very unjust that the innocent should suffer. "'Abdu'l-Bahá shows us how to look at this differently:

> At first sight it may seem very unjust that the innocent should suffer for the guilty, but 'Abdu'l-Bahá assures us that the injustice is only apparent and that, in the long run, perfect justice prevails. He writes: "As to the subject of babes and children and weak ones who are afflicted by the hands of the oppressors ... for those souls there is a recompense in another world ... that suffering is the greatest mercy of God. Verily that mercy of the Lord is far better than all the comfort of this world and the growth and development appertaining to this place of mortality." (Dr. JE Esselmont, *Bahá'u'lláh and the New Era*, p. 96)

We might find ourselves asking:

If God loves me . . .

- why am I still sick?
- why did my child die?
- why am I being abused?
- why can't I find work?
- why did I lose my house?
- why did my spouse leave me?
- why can't I pay my bills?

- why does He let me continually break this law when I don't want to?
- why didn't I get the thing I was praying for?

Thoughts like these lead us to comparing ourselves to others, opening the door to fear (I must have done something truly bad to deserve this punishment); envy and jealousy (why do "they" always seem to get what they want?), fueling the fires of bitterness, causing us to descend into self-pity and allowing us to distance ourselves from the only One who can truly help.

When we can't find answers or don't like the ones we find, we stop believing that God cares about us or worse, we stop believing there is a God at all.

It's our disobedience to God that opens the door to such thinking. Disobedience doesn't have to be a big "sin" like lying (the most odious sin) or backbiting (the most great sin); or a social sin like drinking or having sex outside marriage. It could be something as simple as not reading the Writings morning and evening:

> Recite ye the verses of God every morning and evening. Whoso reciteth them not hath truly failed to fulfil his pledge to the Covenant of God and His Testament and whoso in this day turneth away therefrom, hath indeed turned away from God since time immemorial. Fear ye God, O My servants. (Bahá'u'lláh, *The Kitáb-i-Aqdas*, p. 73, #149)

We might be trying to adhere to all the Writings as best as we can, and still nothing seems to go our way. We still feel guilty, worthless and unacceptable to God. We might feel God is still mad at us for something we did decades ago.

For example, while in the process of going through a divorce, which I initiated, I read:

> ...the partner who is the 'cause of divorce' will 'unquestionably' become the 'victim of formidable calamities'. (Written on behalf of the Universal House of Justice, *Lights of Guidance*, p. 392, #1305)

I never knew if I was the cause of my divorce, but since I certainly had formidable calamities after it, I always thought that this was God's wrath coming down on me, but in fact, it was just the consequences of my actions. All of this changed when I was able to take responsibility for my part in the failure of the marriage, forgive myself, ask God for His forgiveness and believe it had been given.

If we believe that we are praised and chosen by God, the accusation of all the creatures will cause no loss to us:

> Man must seek to gain the acceptance of God and not that of the different classes of men. If one is praised and chosen by God, the accusation of all the creatures will cause no loss to him; and if the man is not accepted in the threshold of God, the praise and admiration of all men will be of no use to him. (*Tablets of 'Abdu'l-Bahá v1*, p. 158)

God does not accuse us, so if we are feeling accused, it's coming from outside ourselves (from others) or inside ourselves (from our lower nature). Judgement and condemnation attack us at our weakest, most vulnerable spot. They might even use quotes from the Writings to punish us, but if we're hearing this, it's not from God. God's Writings might seem harsh, but His voice is always gentle, even when He's correcting us.   His voice is often referred to as a breath or a fragrance – that's how gentle it is! When it's coming from that broken record within, no amount of being obedient or repentant will cause it to go away.

How can we know whether inspiration is coming from God or from our lower nature?

> The question arises: How shall we know whether we are following inspiration from God or satanic promptings of the human soul? Briefly, the point is that in the human material world of phenomena these four are the only existing criteria or avenues of knowledge, and all of them are faulty and unreliable. What then remains? How shall we attain the reality of knowledge? By the breaths and promptings of the Holy Spirit, which is light and knowledge itself. Through it the human mind is quickened and fortified into true conclusions and perfect knowledge. ('Abdu'l-Bahá, *The Promulgation of Universal Peace*, p. 22)

God wants us to like ourselves, and show our true selves to the world:

> Thou art even as a finely tempered sword
> concealed in the darkness of its sheath and its
> value hidden from the artificer's knowledge.
> Wherefore come forth from the sheath of self
> and desire that thy worth may be made
> resplendent and manifest unto all the world.
> (Bahá'u'lláh, *The Hidden Words*, Persian #72)

And to see ourselves as He sees us:

> Rejoice thou with great joy that We have
> remembered thee both now and in the past.
> Indeed the sweet savours of this remembrance
> shall endure and shall not change throughout
> the eternity of the Names of God, the Lord of
> mankind. We have graciously accepted thy
> devotions, thy praise, thy teaching work and the
> services thou hast rendered for the sake of this
> mighty Announcement. We have also hearkened
> unto that which thy tongue hath uttered at the
> meetings and gatherings. Verily thy Lord
> heareth and observest all things. (*Tablets of
> Bahá'u'lláh*, p. 245)

> O thou beloved of my heart! Verily, my soul
> longs for thee, for the lamp of the love of Bahá' is
> lighted within thy heart and I love to look upon
> thy face, for it is glittering with the light of
> guidance among the creatures. Glory be to Him
> who hath united hearts together! (*Tablets of
> 'Abdu'l-Bahá v1*, p. 129)

> Moreover, although these insignificant amounts
> are not worthy of mention, they are well

> pleasing, since the donors offer them for the sake
> of God. If the offering be but a single grain it is
> regarded as the crowning glory of all the
> harvests of the world. (Bahá'u'lláh, *Compilation
> of Compilations v I*, p. 490)

Our lower nature wants us to be isolated and alone.

God created us to be in relationship with Him and with
other people. We need Him and we need each other.

> In his life and being cooperation and association
> are essential. Through association and meeting
> we find happiness and development, individual
> and collective. ('Abdu'l-Bahá, *The Promulgation
> of Universal Peace*, p. 35)

Our lower nature counts on the fact that we will believe
negative thoughts about ourselves, God and others, and
starts to agree with them. So the question is: whose voice
are we going to listen to?

> Shall we not free ourselves from the horror of
> satanic gloom, and hasten towards the rising
> light of the heavenly Beauty? (Bahá'u'lláh, *Kitáb-
> i-Íqán*, p. 38)

As H.M. Balyuzi noted on page 6 of *Edward Granville
Brown and the Bahá'í Faith*, it is important that we take
"sufficient care to sift fact from fiction".

10 RED FLAGS

There are ten things we need to be aware of, which will alert us that we are about to descend into fault-finding, blame and accusation.

1. **Isolating yourself from others**: if you find yourself isolating from other people, it's your lower nature's plan and not the plan of God. You don't have to agree with it. Disagree and get yourself back out there relating to other people.

2. **Suspicious and Mistrustful**: If you find yourself suspicious or distrustful of someone's motives or intent (including your own); or questioning their motives.

    > I have expounded these things for you, for the conservation and protection of the teachings of Bahá'u'lláh, in order that you may be informed, lest any souls shall deceive you and lest any souls shall cause suspicion among you. ('Abdu'l-Bahá, *The Promulgation of Universal Peace*, p. 323-324)

3. **Holding others to their past failures, thoughts, beliefs**; always judging them in terms of the past; never letting them forget that they hurt you or did

something you think was wrong. This is just a waste
of time and energy. Shoghi Effendi tells us to put the
past behind:

> When criticism and harsh words arise within
> a Bahá'í community there is no remedy
> except to put the past behind one and
> persuade all concerned to turn over a new
> leaf, and, for the sake of God and His Faith,
> refrain from mentioning the subjects which
> have led to misunderstanding and
> inharmony.   (Written on behalf of Shoghi
> Effendi, *Lights of Guidance*, p. 94, #324)

Forgive them, give them a chance to take
responsibility for their past. You won't ever be able
to live in the present and have a relationship with
them if you don't forgive their past. How many
times do you forgive? A hundred-thousand:

> . . . if a person falls into errors for a hundred-
> thousand times he may yet turn his face to
> you, hopeful that you will forgive his sins; for
> he must not become hopeless, neither grieved
> nor despondent. This is the conduct and the
> manner of the people of Bahá'. This is the
> foundation of the most high pathway!
> (*Tablets of 'Abdu'l-Bahá v2*, p. 436)

4. **Establishing standards for other people to attain**. If
someone doesn't do what we want or how we want it
done, we accuse them of being selfish or lazy.

For example, sometimes I look at other Bahá'ís who are gossiping and it irritates me. I don't see how they can call themselves Bahá'ís and continually talk about other people. In my mind, I condemn and judge and in my actions, I distance myself from them because I don't want to be their next victim. I myself am trying hard not to backbite, so I assume everyone else is or should be striving to do this too. I forget that there is an ocean to Bahá'u'lláh's revelation, and it's entirely possible that the other person is struggling just as hard as I am, with a different law. Because I've distanced myself from him, I'll never know . . .

5. **Gossip, backbiting and innuendo** all murder a person's reputation with the tongue. "'Abdu'l-Bahá describes what we might find ourselves saying:

> . . . whenever we wish to put on a show of wisdom and learning, of virtue and godliness, we set about mocking and reviling this one and that. "The ideas of such a one," we say, "are wide of the mark, and so-and-so's behavior leaves much to be desired. The religious observances of Zayd are few and far between, and Amr is not firm in his faith. So-and-so's opinions smack of Europe. Fundamentally, Blank thinks of nothing but his own name and fame. Last night when the congregation stood up to pray, the row was out of line, and it is not permissible to follow a different leader. No rich man has died this month, and nothing has been offered to

> charity in memory of the Prophet. ('Abdu'l-
> Bahá, *The Secret of Divine Civilization*, p. 56)

6. **Misunderstanding and accusing others of things that aren't true**. Perhaps someone just didn't understand. This sounds simple but it's very profound. When we make judgments and jump to conclusions, it's generally that we don't have the whole story. We don't have the whole picture, either from someone else or from God.

> In every suffering one can find a meaning
> and a wisdom. But it is not always easy to
> find the secret of that wisdom. It is
> sometimes only when all our suffering has
> passed that we become aware of its
> usefulness. What man considers to be evil
> turns often to be a cause of infinite blessings.
> And this is due to his desire to know more
> than he can. God's wisdom is, indeed,
> inscrutable to us all, and it is no use pushing
> too far trying to discover that which shall
> always remain a mystery to our mind.
> (Shoghi Effendi, *Unfolding Destiny*, p. 434)

For example: as a child I begged God to make the abuse stop, and it didn't, so I stopped believing in God. Years later I realized that I hadn't abused my own child, thereby breaking the cycle of abuse that had been in my family for generations. God had stopped the abuse forever, instead of just in the moment. As a result, it had a much bigger impact. Instead of the abused (me) becoming the abuser; the cycle has been broken for eternity. As a child I misunderstood God's timetable; and the ways in which He answers prayer.

> Often these trials and tests which all Bahá'í Communities inevitably pass through seem terrible, at the moment, but in retrospect we understand that they were due to the frailty of Human nature, to misunderstanding, and to the growing pains which every Bahá'í community must experience. (Written on behalf of Shoghi Effendi, *Lights of Guidance*, p. 602, #2038)

In his introduction to the 1923 compilation *Bahá'í Scriptures*, Horace Holley wrote:

> Day by day the realization deepens in all conscious men and women that in this age new forces are seeking expression - forces so mighty that the difference between understanding and misunderstanding is the immediate crisis between the alternatives of a new, worldwide and spiritualized civilization and a further, even more disastrous undoing of the things that are. It is upon the plane of understanding that the power of the Bahá'í writings operates, in that area of being which lies beyond the personal desire, the personal thought, the personal will. Their operation is to restore in the individual, whatever his race, class, creed, profession or temperament, that eternal vision of the oneness of God whose evolving expression is directly the

development of the soul, and indirectly the
harmonious organization of mankind. (p. v)

7. **Judging others for the same behavior we have
    ourselves** and excusing ourselves while accusing
    others; trying to become a "condemning god" in other
    people's lives; trying to tell them what to do all the
    time; telling them what is wrong with them all the
    time

8. **Tearing down someone else so you will look better**;
    exalting yourself over another

> Know ye not why We created you all from
> the same dust? That no one should exalt
> himself over the other. Ponder at all times in
> your hearts how ye were created. Since We
> have created you all from one same substance
> it is incumbent on you to be even as one soul,
> to walk with the same feet, eat with the same
> mouth and dwell in the same land, that from
> your inmost being, by your deeds and
> actions, the signs of oneness and the essence
> of detachment may be made manifest. Such is
> My counsel to you, O concourse of light!
> Heed ye this counsel that ye may obtain the
> fruit of holiness from the tree of wondrous
> glory. (Bahá'u'lláh, *The Hidden Words*, Arabic
> #68)

> Human society at present exerts a pernicious
> influence upon the soul of man. Instead of
> allowing him to live a life of service and

sacrifice, it is highly competitive and teaches him to pride himself on his accomplishments. From early childhood he is trained to develop his ego and to seek to exalt himself above others, in the ultimate aim of achieving self-importance, success and power. The Revelation of Bahá'u'lláh aims to reverse this process. The soul of man needs to be adorned with the virtues of humility and self-effacement so that it may become detached from the Kingdom of Names. (Adib Taherzadeh, *The Covenant of Bahá'u'lláh*, p. 22)

9. **Self-pity**: If we find ourselves saying things like "poor me", or blaming others and their behavior for our problems, we're probably accusing someone of something, in order to make us the victim.

   Don't confuse feelings with reality. Just because we feel unloved or unlovable because of things others have said about us, does not mean these beliefs are real. If a thought makes us feel bad, it's always coming from the lower nature. It's always a lie, and can be used as a "red flag" to alert us to danger, so we can quickly turn our thoughts around.

10. **Exploiting the weaknesses of others**: Our lower nature uses the weaknesses of others to justify our own righteousness, so we'll often go after the people we know the best. We know the weaknesses of the people we spend the most time with. For example, you might find yourself saying things like: "Look at

how wrong my spouse is. She never . . . (fill in the blank); He always . . . (fill in the blank).

If someone else's behaviour bothers you that much, you probably have that trait too, which is why Bahá'u'lláh tells us:

> . . . magnify not the faults of others that thine own faults may not appear great . . .
> (Bahá'u'lláh, *The Hidden Words*, Persian #44)

The fault we accuse others of having, we probably have as well and just aren't seeing it.

An expression that always helps me is to remember that when I'm pointing a finger at someone else, there are 3 fingers pointing back at me (try it right now – point your finger and look at the 3 fingers folded into the palm of your hand, pointing back at you!) In this way, you can use the faults of others to shine a light on your own; to bring you back to focusing on your own faults.

> Whenever you recognize the fault of another, think of yourself! What are my imperfections? -- and try to remove them. Do this whenever you are tried through the words or deeds of others. Thus you will grow, become more perfect. You will overcome self, you will not even have time to think of the faults of others... ('Abdul-Bahá, *Star of the West*', v8, No. 10, p 138)

Know the truth and don't waste time with strife. We don't have to be accused and condemned by ourselves or others anymore. The Bahá'í Writings tell us quite clearly not to give offense or take offence.

> The members of an Assembly must learn to express their views frankly, calmly, without passion or rancour. They must also learn to listen to the opinions of their fellow members without taking offence or belittling the views of another. Bahá'í consultation is not an easy process. It requires love, kindliness, moral courage and humility. Thus no member should ever allow himself to be prevented from expressing frankly his view because it may offend a fellow member; and, realizing this, no member should take offence at another member's statements. (Universal House of Justice, *Lights of Guidance*, p.180, #590)

The only person's opinion who matters is God's.

> To be approved of God alone should be one's aim. ('Abdu'l-Bahá, *Lights of Guidance*, p. 33, #120)

> Seeking the approval of men is many times the cause of imperilling the approval of God. ('Abdu'l-Bahá, *Star of the West, v6, No. 6*, p.45)

WHY IS IT DETRIMENTAL?

Many people live under a perpetual pile of fault-finding, blame and accusation which, when we buy into the lies told to us or told by us, can breed envy and jealousy. We find ourselves resenting or hating others because they have something we like and don't have. It tears us down and robs us of our faith and confidence in ourselves. It robs us of our dignity. We doubt our own worth and forget our nobility.   It makes us feel like second class citizens in the Kingdom of God because we believe that we're "no good", "not good enough" and "can't do anything right". It keeps us from our true destiny, which is to "know and worship God". It makes us feel guilty (whether or not we are), condemned, ashamed of our behaviour, worthless and unclean. It leaves us feeling totally hopeless and unable to see a way out. It makes us want to give up. Sometimes we do, and life stops; we stop trying; and we can't imagine anything good will ever come our way again. We retreat into depression and addictions.

We assume that everything will be the same in the present and the future, as it was in the past. We believe we are the cause of our calamities, and that we deserve to be punished. It traps us in the prison of self and throws away the key, and we don't even know life could be any different.

Listening to these thoughts keeps us from becoming who God created us to be, which opens the door to disease. Our thoughts turn against us and eventually our bodies conform to our thoughts and turns against us also.

> Sometimes if the nervous system is paralyzed through fear, a spiritual remedy is necessary . . . It often happens that sorrow makes one ill. (*'Abdu'l-Bahá in London*, p. 65)

> Fear, anger, worry, etcetera, are very prejudicial to health. (Dr. J.E. Esslemont, *Bahá'u'lláh and the New Era*, p. 108)

Fault-finding, blame and accusation keep us from healing and from having a peaceful, joyful life in God.

> In the hearts of men no real love is found, and the condition is such that, unless their susceptibilities are quickened by some power so that unity, love and accord may develop within them, there can be no healing ('Abdu'l-Bahá, *The Promulgation of Universal Peace*, p. 171)

When we believe the lies; we isolate from God (forgetting to pray, read the Writings and participate in Bahá'í Community life). We isolate from ourselves (through addictions) and from others (through estrangement and divorce), believing we can't be forgiven. This keeps us from intimacy and ultimately ensures that we don't have peaceful communications with anybody.

In the article on Fault-Finding in the blog "Living Life Fully"[4], the author (unknown) says:

> When we find fault in something that someone else has done, we're very often adding a negative element to our relationship with that person. We're defining limits of trust and sharing--if I know that someone is going to find fault with everything that I do, I will not share with that person unless I'm truly seeking criticism. As fewer people are willing to share with us, we lose much of the richness that comes from and through that sharing, and we become more isolated, less integrated. The loss of the sharing of others is one of the greatest losses we can cause ourselves, and it may even reach a point at which people just don't want to be around us at all.
>
> Fault-finding and criticizing, no matter what our intentions, tend to drive wedges between us and other people. A person who finds fault in everything is a person to be avoided, when all is said and done, and who among us wants other people to avoid us whenever they can?

Separation from others could take the form of estrangement, divorce, moving away from family, friends or our Bahá'í communities. 'Abdu'l-Bahá tells us:

---

[4] http://www.livinglifefully.com/faultfinding.htm

> Souls are liable to estrangement. ('Abdu'l-Bahá,
> Tablets of 'Abdu'l-Bahá v2, p. 391)

When we become estranged, we are set up for others to
accuse us. We hear their condemnation, believe it; take it
in, collapse into it, agree with it, which causes a further
breach.

For example, when on the advice of my therapist and with
guidance from the House of Justice, I wrote a letter to my
parents, letting them know that I remembered what had
been done to me as a child, my mother (bitterly divorced
from my father for 16 years) drove half way across the
country to meet with him to discuss the letters. They
invited my brothers and ex-husband to a "family meeting"
to have me declared crazy and to remove my son from my
care. Fortunately, my ex refused to attend, saying he
didn't believe that I was crazy or that my son was in any
danger, but my brothers have remained estranged from
me to this day. For years I was in torment: did I make it
up or didn't I? My parents went to their graves, and still I
had no answers save what was in my heart, and the
anxiety kept me from being able to work in paid
employment for 20 years.

God doesn't want us to be estranged. He wants us to be in
fellowship with each other. He wants us to work together
in groups. Everything is done in groups in this Faith –
from the Core Activities; to the Assemblies; to marriage
and family life – God loves those who work in groups.

As we see in the following quote, there are huge
advantages!

Whensoever holy souls, drawing on the powers of heaven, shall arise with such qualities of the spirit, and march in unison, rank on rank, every one of those souls will be even as one thousand, and the surging waves of that mighty ocean will be even as the battalions of the Concourse on high.

What a blessing that will be -- when all shall come together, even as once separate torrents, rivers and streams, running brooks and single drops, when collected together in one place will form a mighty sea. And to such a degree will the inherent unity of all prevail, that the traditions, rules, customs and distinctions in the fanciful life of these populations will be effaced and vanish away like isolated drops, once the great sea of oneness doth leap and surge and roll.

I swear by the Ancient Beauty, that at such a time overwhelming grace will so encircle all, and the sea of grandeur will so overflow its shores, that the narrowest strip of water will grow wide as an endless sea, and every merest drop will be even as the shoreless deep.

O ye loved ones of God! Struggle and strive to reach that high station, and to make a splendour so to shine across these realms of earth that the rays of it will be reflected back from a dawning-point on the horizon of eternity. This is the very foundation of the Cause of God. This is the very pith of the Law of God. This is the mighty structure raised up by the Manifestations of God.

> This is why the orb of God's world dawneth.
> This is why the Lord establisheth Himself on the
> throne of His human body. ('Abdu'l-Bahá,
> *Selections from the Writings of 'Abdu'l-Bahá*, pp.
> 260-261)

When we judge others, we can no longer feel compassion
or empathy. In his book "Love Beyond Reason", John
Ortberg says:

> When we judge people, we feel less of an
> obligation to suffer with and for them. When we
> judge people, we cease to pay attention to them.
> (John Ortberg, *Love Beyond Reason*, p. 35)

Remember, thoughts lead to actions. If you start believing
what your accusers tell you, you will begin making
choices that are less than noble, and it will become a self-
fulfilling prophecy.

For example, as a small child, I heard my mother say: "I
wish she'd never been born." It was said in a moment of
frustration and I'm sure now, that she didn't mean it. But
as a child, I took it to heart, and believed it. If my mother
didn't want me, who else would? It affected my ability to
make friends; to sustain any long-term relationships; and
kept me from dating. It turned me away from God and for
many years (before finding the Bahá'í Faith), I even
became an atheist. My mother's "emotional abuse" had a
lasting effect because I took offence when none was meant.
The abuse I perpetrated on myself as a result of that belief
lasted for 54 years. When I finally understood this, I was
able to detach, forgive myself, ask God for His forgiveness
and move on with my life, with a new awareness of the

truth that she didn't set out to destroy me; and that God's love was with me all along. It was me who moved, not God.

When we're separated from God, we also lose out on His love, His Words and His fellowship. We stop doing the things He's asked us to do. Veil after veil comes between us and God till it's so thick that we can't hear His voice or feel His love anymore. We forget to turn to Him first in times of trouble and may even turn away from our Faith, and are prevented from knowing the person God created us to be.

If we don't walk in God's ways, we're trapped inside the prison of self and listening to the wrong voice. This is not a place we want to be!

'Abdu'l-Bahá tells us:

> Alas for them! They have deluded themselves
> with a fable, and to indulge their appetites they
> have done away with their own selves. They
> gave up everlasting glory in exchange for human
> pride, and they sacrificed greatness in both
> worlds to the demands of the insistent self.
> (*Selections from the Writings of 'Abdu'l-Bahá*, p.
> 259)

As long as we stay in the prison of self, God can't reach us or help us out. We have to meet Him half way and turn to Him first.

Release comes by making of the will a Door through which the confirmations of the Spirit come. (*'Abdu'l-Bahá in London*, p. 120)

10 THINGS WE CAN DO INSTEAD

But how are we told to treat our enemies? Bahá'u'lláh sets the standard for us, and His standard is very high. We need to know what it is:

> They have sympathy even for the enemies and are faithful friends even to the unjust   (*Tablets of 'Abdu'l-Bahá v2*, p. 400)

> You must consider your enemies as your friends, look upon your evil-wishers as your well-wishers and treat them accordingly. ('Abdu'l-Bahá, *The Promulgation of Universal Peace*, p. 453)

> Ye have heard that it hath been said, 'Thou shalt love thy neighbor, and thou shalt not vex thine enemy with enmity.' But I say unto you, love your enemies, bless them that curse you, do good to them that hate you, and pray for them which despitefully use you, and persecute you; that ye may be the children of your Father which is in heaven: for He maketh His sun to rise on the evil and on the good, and sendeth down the rain of His mercy on the just and on the unjust. ('Abdu'l-Bahá, *The Secret of Divine Civilization*, p. 81)

Consider the example of 'Abdul-Bahá, in this story told by Howard Colby Ives:

I remember as though it were yesterday another illustration of 'Abdu'l-Bahá's divine technique. I was not at all well that summer. A relapse was threatening a return of a condition which had necessitated a major operation the year before. My nervous condition made me consider breaking the habit of smoking which had been with me all my adult life. I had always prided myself on the ability to break the habit at any time. In fact I had several times cut off the use of tobacco for a period of many months. But this time to my surprise and chagrin I found my nerves and will in such a condition that after two or three days the craving became too much for me. Finally it occurred to me to ask the assistance of 'Abdu'l-Bahá. I had read His beautiful Tablet beginning: "0 ye pure friends of God!" in which He glorified personal cleanliness and urged the avoidance of anything tending towards habits of self-indulgence. "Surely," I said to myself, "He will tell me how to overcome this habit."

So, when I next saw Him I told Him all about it. It was like a child confessing to His mother, and my voice trailed away to embarrassed silence after only the fewest of words. But He understood, indeed much better than I did. Again I was conscious of an embracing, understanding love as He regarded me. After a moment He asked quietly, how much I smoked. I told him. He said He did not think that would hurt me, that the men in the Orient smoked all the time, that their hair and beards and clothing became saturated, and often very offensive. But that I did not do this, and at my age and having been accustomed to it for so many years He did not think that I should let it trouble me at all. His gentle eyes and smile seemed to hold a twinkle that recalled my impression of His enjoyment of a divine joke.

I was somewhat overwhelmed. Not a dissertation on the evils of habit; not an explanation of the bad effects on health; not a summoning of my will power to overcome desire, rather a Charter of Freedom did He present to me. I did not understand but it was a great relief for somehow I knew that this was wise advice. So immediately that inner conflict was stilled and I enjoyed my smoke with no smitings of conscience. But two days after this conversation I found the desire for tobacco had entirely left me and I did not smoke again for seven years. (Howard Colby Ives, *Portals to Freedom*, p. 45)

Now that we know how detrimental fault-finding, blame and accusation are; and we know the standard we are striving towards, we can more easily demolish the idols of our own idle fancy, plant the standard of Divine guidance in our hearts, disentangle our minds from the things we believed in the past, and hasten, free and untrammelled, to the shores of eternal salvation.

His beloved Master, called upon him to demolish those idols which his own idle fancy had carved and to plant upon their shattered fragments the standard of Divine guidance. He appealed to him to disentangle his mind from the fettering creeds of the past, and to hasten,

> free and untrammelled, to the shores of eternal
> salvation. (Nabil, *The Dawn-Breakers*, p. 266)

We can be set free from fault-finding and blame and
regain victory over ourselves if we follow these ten steps:

1. **Know that we have a choice:**

   > If we think "he hates me", the world would tell us to
   > hate him back.

   > If she hits me, we learn to hit her back.

   > God wants us to behave differently. Blindly
   > following the example we were taught is imitation
   > and to be avoided at all costs:

   > > We must discover for ourselves where and
   > > what reality is. In religious beliefs nations
   > > and peoples today are imitators of ancestors
   > > and forefathers. If a man's father was a
   > > Christian, he himself is a Christian; a
   > > Buddhist is the son of a Buddhist, a
   > > Zoroastrian of a Zoroastrian. A gentile or an
   > > idolator follows the religious footsteps of his
   > > father and ancestry. This is absolute
   > > imitation. The requirement in this day is that
   > > man must independently and impartially
   > > investigate every form of reality. (Abdu'l-
   > > Baha, *The Promulgation of Universal Peace*, p.
   > > 327)

   > 'Abdu'l-Bahá promises us:

If we abandon these timeworn blind
imitations and investigate reality, all of us
will be unified. No discord will remain;
antagonism will disappear. All will associate
in fellowship. All will enjoy the cordial bonds
of friendship. The world of creation will then
attain composure. The dark and gloomy
clouds of blind imitations and dogmatic
variances will be scattered and dispelled; the
Sun of Reality will shine most gloriously.
('Abdu'l-Bahá, *The Promulgation of Universal
Peace*, pp. 344-345)

We have to make a choice about which Kingdom
we're going to serve: God's Word, or the promptings
of our lower nature? With God, all things are
possible and we can make changes in the way we
react to things. We can discern the faults of others
but not condemn them.

2. **Turn towards God**

Against calumny there is no defence . . .
having no helper, assistant nor shelter from
the sword of accusation and the teeth of
calumny, save God! (*Tablets of 'Abdu'l-Bahá
v2*, p. 379)

The Master said: turn your back to the
darkness and your face to Me. (Written on
behalf of Shoghi Effendi, *Unfolding Destiny*, p.
457)

> We supplicate God that He may destroy the
> veils which limit our vision and that these
> becloudings which darken the way of the
> manifestation of the shining lights may be
> dispelled in order that the effulgent Sun of
> Reality may shine forth. We implore and
> invoke God, seeking His assistance and
> confirmation. ('Abdu'l-Bahá, *The
> Promulgation of Universal Peace*, p. 294)

3. **Focus on God and not on our own personal battles**

It's hard to feel close to other people – the distance
between us is too great, but if we each walk with God
and follow His teachings, we'll automatically draw
closer to each other.

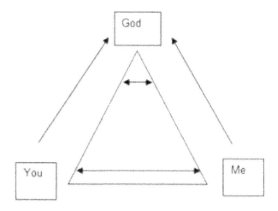

As we see in the diagram, "you and me" are far apart,
and no amount of good-will on our part will bring us
close together. When each of us gets closer to God,
though, we automatically draw closer to each other.

4. **Immerse ourselves in the Writings and be programmed by God's word.** We have to know the Word of God so we can discern truth from error; recognize thoughts that are not from Him, and don't get caught up in lies. We need to be constantly vigilant so we can catch the thoughts before they take hold and do their damage.

> It demands daily vigilance in the control of one's carnal desires and corrupt inclinations. (Shoghi Effendi: *The Advent of Divine Justice*, p. 30)

The best way to retrain our thought processes with God's truth is through immersing ourselves in the Ocean of His Words. When we renew our minds and replace old modes of thinking with new, God's Word will teach us what's from Him and what's from our lower natures.

God is the only one able to convict someone of sin. To know what is acceptable before God or not, we have the Writings to turn to. They make us want to do better; be better; they strengthen our relationship with God; they make us feel hopeful, positive and longing to change.

We can trust that the thoughts that come to us from God are always based in the Word of God; but when they come from ourselves, they're based on our own experiences and decisions, and come from an unrenewed mind. When our minds are continually being renewed through reading the Writings morning and eve, we will be in a much better position to discern where our thoughts are coming from.

5. **Make every thought captive** so we can discern whether it's arising from God or from our lower natures; and use the Words of God to drown out the idle fancies and vain imaginings. Put a "stop sign" in our brain. When we have a thought, pause, count to 10 – 20 – 50 if necessary, then ask where this thought came from. Is it from God or from our lower nature? Should we give it voice? Remember:

> Not everything that a man knoweth can be disclosed, nor can everything that he can disclose be regarded as timely, nor can every timely utterance be considered as suited to the capacity of those who hear it. (*Gleanings from the Writings of Bahá'u'lláh*, p. 176)

6. **Abstain from Fault-finding:**

> Each of us is responsible for one life only, and that is our own. Each of us is immeasurably far from being "perfect as our Heavenly Father is perfect: and the task of perfecting our own life and character is one that requires all our attention, our will-power and energy... On no subject are the Bahá'í teachings more emphatic that on the necessity to abstain from fault-finding, while being ever eager to discover and root out our own faults and overcome our own failings.

(Written on behalf of Shoghi Effendi, *Lights of Guidance*, p. 91, #311)

7. **Listen to our elders:**

    What the believers need is not only . . . to really study the teachings, but also to have more peace-makers circulating among them. Unfortunately, not only average people, but average Bahá'ís, are very immature; gossip, trouble-making, criticism, seem easier than the putting into practice of love, constructive words and cooperation. It is one of the functions of the older and the more mature Bahá'ís, to help the weaker ones to iron out their difficulties and learn to really function and live like true believers! (Written on behalf of Shoghi Effendi, *Lights of Guidance*, p. 90, #310)

8. **Follow the example of those who have endured every tribulation and calamity**

    Gird up thy loins, strengthen thy back, be not discouraged or grieved if people are pouring the arrows of scorn and blame thee, in so much as in this thou wilt follow the example of those who have endured every tribulation and calamity. (*Tablets of 'Abdu'l-Bahá v2*, p. 281-282)

9. **Don't listen to negative voices:** Bahá'u'lláh tells us not to be kind to a "liar, traitor or thief", so we don't

have to listen to these negative voices. We don't have
to give them room in our heads.

> Kindness cannot be shown the tyrant, the
> deceiver, or the thief, because, far from
> awakening them to the error of their ways, it
> maketh them to continue in their perversity
> as before. No matter how much kindliness ye
> may expend upon the liar, he will but lie the
> more, for he believeth you to be deceived,
> while ye understand him but too well, and
> only remain silent out of your extreme
> compassion. (*Selections from the Writings of
> Abdu'l-Baha*, p. 158)

We can tell the difference between the voice of God
and the voice of our lower nature, because, as
Bahá'u'lláh tells us:

> Every good thing is of God, and every evil
> thing is from yourselves. Will ye not
> comprehend? (*Gleanings from the Writings of
> Bahá'u'lláh*, p. 149)

10. **Be silent against accusations:** This is hard to do! We
    want to protect ourselves and protect our reputations;
    to show that the other person is at fault.

    When you're trying to break this habit of fault-
    finding and blame, you may need to zip your mouth
    and don't make any comments at all, and that's to be
    encouraged. Remember, the Báb set the standard for

what we should speak about when He gave us this
prayer:

> I beg Thee to forgive me, O my Lord, for
> every mention but the mention of Thee, and
> for every praise but the praise of Thee, and
> for every delight but delight in Thy nearness,
> and for every pleasure but the pleasure of
> communion with Thee, and for every joy but
> the joy of Thy love and of Thy good-pleasure,
> and for all things pertaining unto me which
> bear no relationship unto Thee, O Thou Who
> art the Lord of lords, He Who provideth the
> means and unlocketh the doors. (The Báb,
> *Bahá'í Prayers*, p. 79)

And Bahá'u'lláh reminds us:

> He must . . . observe silence and refrain from
> idle talk. For the tongue is a smoldering fire,
> and excess of speech a deadly poison.
> (Bahá'u'lláh, *The Kitáb-i-Íqán*, p.193)

Let's take back our peace! It's worth the hard work!

CONCLUSION

Our battle is not with other people, it's with our lower nature.

When you've recognized all of the people and situations in your life where fault-finding, blame and accusation are present, go before God; talk to Him about it; take responsibility for your part and ask God's forgiveness, trusting it will be forgiven. Ask God's help in detaching so you won't get caught up in it again, and then thank Him for His mercy and bounties.

Here is a meditation you can use to remove fault-finding and blame:

> Fault-finding and blame, I take responsibility for you, and I detach myself from the hold they have on me from blindly following what past generations have taught me.

> I take responsibility for all the bitterness coming out of blaming others and having them blame me, and I ask God to remove this from me.

> I take responsibility for all the times I've given or taken offence, and I ask God to forgive me for all of them.

I let go of all comparisons and competition I've had with other people, and the envy and jealousy which ensued, and I beg God to forgive me for all of them.

I take responsibility over suspicion and mistrust and ask God to replace them with faith, trust, hope and love.

I take responsibility over all fear and ask God's help to detach from all the ways it has hold of me.

I take responsibility for all judgments and criticism I've held towards God, others and myself, and I ask God to transmute them into peacefulness and love.

I take responsibility for all the lies I believed, emanating from my lower nature, and from others, and I ask God to shine the light of truthfulness on all of them.

I take authority for all the times I've tried to be perfect, thinking that I knew what was best and forcing my will on my life and on others. Please God, forgive me for not trusting that Your Way was better.

Please God, forgive me for all of it; and from now on, guide my steps aright through Thine inspiration.

Now, make a list of everyone and every situation which the following sins suggest.

- Self-exaltation
- Self-condemnation
- Guilt

- Gossip and slander
- Confusion
- Racism and bigotry in yourself and in your family tree
- Envy and jealousy
- Scapegoating and victimization
- Division and strife
- Betrayal and grief stored in every cell of your being
- Rebellion, control and manipulation
- Misunderstanding
- Unworthiness
- Shame
- Isolation
- Self-pity
- Deceit
- Torment and despair
- Fear
- Accusation against God, yourself and others

If you'd like, find a stone to represent each instance, and when you're ready, take responsibility for every situation, letting go of the stones one by one; asking God to help you detach from them all; then put on God's armor and protection against them ever coming back to destroy your life again.

God, I ask your forgiveness for each offence; and I forgive myself for all of them as well. Thank you, God, for removing these from me; and for your forgiveness and mercy. (Adapted from a talk given in the *"For My Life Online"* course by Henry Wright: For My Life Online[5])

---

[5] http://www.beinhealth.com/oj/bihprograms/for-my-life-wow/

MEDITATIONS TO RELEASE AND LET GO OF ALL FORMS OF CRITICISM

I call on Thee, O Unfastener, O Deliver, O Healer! [6]

Thou dost perceive my tears and the sighs I utter, and hearest my groaning, and my wailing, and the lamentation of my heart. By Thy might! My trespasses have kept me back from drawing nigh unto Thee; and my sins have held me far from the court of Thy holiness.

Thou hast inspired my soul to offer its supplication to Thee, and but for Thee, I would not call upon Thee. I yield Thee praise inasmuch as Thou didst reveal Thyself unto me, and I beg Thee to forgive me, since I have fallen short in my duty to know Thee and have failed to walk in the path of Thy love.[7]

Thy love, O my Lord, hath enriched me, and separation from Thee hath destroyed me, and remoteness from Thee hath consumed me.[8]

---

6 Baha'u'llah, The Long Healing Prayer
[7] The Báb, Baha'i Prayers, p. 63
[8] Bahá'u'lláh, Long Obligatory Prayer, Baha'i Prayers, p. 12

I am a captive; rid me of my bondage, by the power
of Thy might and through the force of Thy will, that I
may soar on the wings of detachment towards the
loftiest summits of Thy creation.[9]

I beg of Thee to wash away my sins as befitteth Thy
Lordship, and to[10] grant forgiveness unto me and
unto my father and my mother.[11] I beseech Thee
with all the ardor of my invocation to pardon
whosoever hath hurt me, forgive him that hath
conspired against me and offended me, and wash
away the misdeeds of them that have wrought
injustice upon me. Vouchsafe unto them Thy goodly
gifts, give them joy, relieve them from sorrow, grant
them peace and prosperity, give them Thy bliss and
pour upon them Thy bounty.[12]

Grant that I may, at all times and under all
conditions, lay hold on thy cord, and be rid of all
attachment to anyone except Thee, and may keep
mine eyes directed towards the horizon of Thy
Revelation, and may carry out what Thou hast
prescribed unto me in Thy Tablets.[13]

Keep me safe, then, from whatsoever may be
abhorrent unto Thee, and graciously assist me to obey
Thee, and to shun whatsoever may stir up any evil or
corrupt desire within me.[14] Blot out from my heart all

---

[9] Baha'u'llah, Prayers and Meditations by Baha'u'llah, p. 103

[10] The Báb, Baha'i Prayers, p. 63

[11] Bahá'u'lláh, Tablets of Bahá'u'lláh, pp. 24-25.

[12] The Will and Testament of 'Abdul-Bahá, p. 19

[13] Bahá'u'lláh, Baha'i Prayers, p. 48

[14] Bahá'u'lláh, Baha'i Prayers, p. 48

idle fancies and vain imaginings.[15] Fix, then, mine eyes upon Thee, and rid me of all attachment to aught else except Thyself.[16]

Help me then to quaff, O my God, from the fingers of mercy the living waters of Thy loving-kindness, that I may utterly forget all else except Thee, and be occupied only with Thy Self. [17]

Deliver me from the ills that have encircled me, and wash me thoroughly with the waters of thy graciousness and mercy, and attire me with the raiment of wholesomeness, through Thy forgiveness and bounty.[18] Write down, then, for me the good of this world and of the world to come.[19]

Powerful art Thou to do what pleaseth Thee. Thou art, verily, the All-Powerful, the Most Generous.[20]

---

[15] Bahá'u'lláh, Baha'i Prayers, p. 49
[16] Bahá'u'lláh, Baha'i Prayers, p. 88
[17] Prayers and Meditations by Baha'u'llah, p. 30
[18] Bahá'u'lláh, Bahá'í World Faith, p. 145.
[19] Bahá'u'lláh, Baha'i Prayers, p. 53
[20] Bahá'u'lláh, Baha'i Prayers, p. 52

BIBLIOGRAPHY

WORKS OF THE BÁB

Selections from the Writings of the Báb. Haifa: Bahá'í World Centre, 1982.

WORKS OF BAHÁ'U'LLÁH

Gleanings from the Writings of Bahá'u'lláh. Trans. Shoghi Effendi. Wilmette: Baha'i Publishing Trust, 1983.

The Hidden Words of Baha'u'llah. Wilmette: Baha'i Publishing Trust, 1975.

The Kitáb-i-Aqdas.   Haifa: Bahá'í World Centre, 1992.

The Kitáb-i-Íqán. Wilmette: Baha'i Publishing Trust, 1983.

Prayers and Meditations by Bahá'u'lláh. Trans. Shoghi Effendi. Wilmette: Bahá'í Publishing Trust, 1987.

Tablets of Baha'u'llah Revealed After the Kitáb-i-Aqdas. Wilmette: Baha'i Publishing Trust, 1988.

WORKS OF 'ABDU'L-BAHÁ

Abdu'l-Bahá in London. Oakham: UK Bahá'í Publishing Trust, 1982.

Foundations of World Unity. Wilmette: Baha'i Publishing Trust, 1968.

Paris Talks. London: Baha'i Publishing Trust, 1995.

The Promulgation of Universal Peace. Wilmette: Baha'i Publishing Trust, 1982.

The Secret of Divine Civilization. Wilmette: US Bahá'í Publishing Trust, 1990.

Selections from the Writings of 'Abdu'l-Bahá. Haifa: Bahá'í World Centre, 1978.

Tablets of 'Abdu'l-Bahá Abbas, v1. Chicago: Bahá'í Publishing Society, 1909.

The Will and Testament of 'Abdu'l-Bahá

WORKS OF SHOGHI EFFENDI

The Advent of Divine Justice. Wilmette: US Bahá'í Publishing Trust, 1990.

Bahá'í Administration. Wilmette: US Bahá'í Publishing Trust, 1974.

Light of Divine Guidance, v1. Hofheim-Langenhain: Bahá'í Publishing Trust of Germany (Bahá'í-Verlag), 1985.

Messages to the Antipodes. Mona Vale: Bahá'í Publications Australia, 1997.

Unfolding Destiny. Oakham: UK Bahá'í Publishing Trust, 1981.

WORKS OF THE UNIVERSAL HOUSE OF JUSTICE

Messages from the Universal House of Justice: 1963 to 1986. Wilmette: Bahá'í Publishing Trust, 1996.

COMPILATIONS

Baha'i Prayers. The Báb, Bahá'u'lláh, and 'Abdu'l-Bahá. Wilmette: Baha'i Publishing Trust, 2002.

Baha'i World Faith, Bahá'u'lláh and 'Abdu'l-Bahá. Wilmette: Bahá'í Publishing Trust, 1943.

Bahíyyih Khánum: The Greatest Holy Leaf, Bahá'u'lláh, 'Abdu'l-Bahá, Shoghi Effendi and The Greatest Holy Leaf. Haifa: Bahá'í World Centre, 1982

The Compilation of Compilations, v I, Bahá'u'lláh, 'Abdu'l-Bahá, and Shoghi Effendi. Maryborough: Bahá'í Publications Australia, 1991.

The Divine Art of Living. The Báb, Bahá'u'lláh, and 'Abdu'l-Bahá. Wilmette: Baha'i Publishing, 2006.

Homosexuality, Bahá'u'lláh, Shoghi Effendi, and The Universal House of Justice. 1993, Bahá'í Library Online.

Lights of Guidance: A Baha'i Reference File. Hornby, Helen, comp. and ed. New Delhi: Baha'i Publishing Trust, 1994.

Quickeners of Mankind. The Báb, Bahá'u'lláh, 'Abdu'l-Bahá, Shoghi Effendi and the Universal House of Justice.

The National Spiritual Assembly of the Bahá'ís of Canada, 1980.

STATEMENTS BY THE BAHÁ'Í INTERNATIONAL COMMUNITY

Creating Violence Free Families. New York: A summary report of a Symposium on Strategies for Creating Violence-Free Families, initiated by the Baha'i International Community and co-sponsored by the United Nations Children's Fund (UNICEF), and the United Nations Development Fund for Women (UNIFEM), 23 May 1994.

Who is Writing the Future? Wilmette: Bahá'í Publishing Trust, February, 1999

OTHER BAHÁ'Í SOURCES

http://bahai-library.com

http://bahai-education.org/

Ocean database.

Balyuzi, H.M. Abdu'l-Baha: The Centre of the Covenant. Oxford: George Ronald, 1971.

Edward Granville Browne and the Bahá'í Faith. London: George Ronald, 1970.

Blomfield, Lady. The Chosen Highway. Oxford: George Ronald, 2007.

Esslemont, Dr. J.E. Baha'u'llah and the New Era. Wilmette: US Bahá'í Publishing Trust, 1980

Faizí, Abu'l-Qásim. Conqueror of Hearts: Excerpts from Letters, Talks, and Writings of Hand of the Cause of God Abu'l-Qásim Faizí. Ed.Shirley Macias. 2002. Bahá'í Library Online.

Gail, Marzieh. The Sheltering Branch. Oxford: George Ronald, 1959.

Gammage, Susan. Violence and Abuse: Reasons and Remedies. New Delhi: Baha'i Publishing Trust, 2009.

Honnold, Annamarie. Vignettes from the Life of 'Abdu'l-Bahá. Oxford: George Ronald, 1991.

Hollinger, Richard (ed). Abdul-Baha in America: Agnes Parsons' Diary. Los Angeles: Kalimat Press, 1996.

Ives, Howard Colby. Portals to Freedom. Oxford: George Ronald, 1983.

Nabil-i-A'zam. Dawn-Breakers: Nabil's Narrative of the Early Days of the Baha'i Revelation. Wilmette: Bahá'í Publishing Trust, 1932

National Spiritual Assembly of the Baha'is of the United States. Developing Distinctive Baha'i Communities: Guidelines for Spiritual Assemblies. Wilmette: Baha'i Publishing Trust, 1998.

Star of the West, vols. 4, 6, 8. Chicago: National Spiritual Assembly of the United States, 1911.

Taherzadeh, Adib. The Revelation of Bahá'u'lláh v 4. Oxford: George Ronald, 1976.

The Covenant of Baha'u'llah. Oxford: George Ronald, 1992.

OTHER SOURCES

Ortberg, John. Love Beyond Reason. Peabody, MA : Zondervan, 2001.

ABOUT THE AUTHOR

 Susan Gammage is a Bahá'í-inspired author, educator and researcher with a passion for finding ways to help people apply Bahá'í principles to everyday life situations so they can learn to "live the life". She has published over 600 articles and twelve books and nothing gives her greater pleasure than working on a whole lot more. She is blessed to be able to live in one of the most beautiful parts of Canada.

You can find her on the web at www.susangammage.com

Printed in Great Britain
by Amazon